Rhymes a la Mode

Andrew Lang

Contents

Rhymes a la Mode	7
BALLADE DEDICATORY--TO MRS. ELTON OF WHITE STAUNTON	7
L'ENVOI--To E. W. G.	13
A VISION IN THE STRAND	14
ALMAE MATRES--(ST. ANDREWS,	18
1862. OXFORD, 1865)	18
DESIDERIUM--IN MEMORIAM S. F. A.	20
BALLADE OF MIDDLE AGE	21
THE LAST CAST--THE ANGLER'S APOLOGY	22
TWILIGHT--SONNET (AFTER RICHEPIN)	24
BALLADE OF SUMMER--TO C. H. ARKCOLL	25
BALLADE OF CHRISTMAS GHOSTS	26
LOVE'S EASTER--SONNET	27
BALLADE OF THE GIRTON GIRL	28
RONSARD'S GRAVE	29
SAN TERENZO	31
ROMANCE	32
BALLADE OF HIS OWN COUNTRY	33
TO C. H. ARKCOLL	33
VILLANELLE--(To M. Joseph Boulmier, author of "Les Villanelles.")	34
TRIOLETS AFTER MOSCHUS	35
BALLADE OF CRICKET--TO T. W. LANG	36
THE LAST MAYING	37
HOMERIC UNITY	40
IN TINTAGEL	40
PISIDICE	42
FROM THE EAST TO THE WEST	43
LOVE THE VAMPIRE [Greek text]	44
BALLADE OF THE BOOK-MAN'S PARADISE	45
BALLADE OF A FRIAR	47
BALLADE OF NEGLECTED MERIT {1}	48
BALLADE OF RAILWAY NOVELS	49
THE CLOUD CHORUS (FROM ARISTOPHANES)	50
BALLADE OF LITERARY FAME	52
A VERY WOFUL BALLADE OF THE ART CRITIC (TO E. A. ABBEY.)	54
ART'S MARTYR	55
THE PALACE O BRIC-A-BRAC	57
RONDEAUX OF THE GALLERIES	59
THE BARBAROUS BIRD-GODS:	60
A SAVAGE PARABASIS	60
MAN AND THE ASCIDIAN--A MORALITY	62
BALLADE OF THE PRIMITIVE JEST	64
CAMEOS--SONNETS FROM THE ANTIQUE	65
CAMEOS	65
HELEN ON THE WALLS--(Iliad, iii. 146.)	66
THE ISLES OF THE BLESSED	67
DEATH--(AEsch., Fr., 156.)	68
COLONUS--(OEd. Col., 667-705.)	69
THE PASSING OF OEDIPOUS--(OEd. Col., 1655-1666.)	70
THE TAMING OF TYRO--(Soph., Fr., 587.)	71
TO ARTEMIS--(Hippol., Eurip., 73-87.)	72

CRITICISM OF LIFE--(Hippol, Eurip .P., 252-266.) 73
AMARYLLIS--(Theocritus, Idyll, iii.) 73
THE CANNIBAL ZEUS--A.D. 160 74
INVOCATION OF ISIS--(Apuleius, Metamorph. XI.) 75
THE COMING OF ISIS 75
THE SPINET 76
Notes: 80

RHYMES A LA MODE

BY
Andrew Lang

Rhymes a la Mode

BALLADE DEDICATORY--TO MRS. ELTON OF WHITE STAUNTON

The painted Briton built his mound,
And left his celts and clay,
On yon fair slope of sunlit ground
That fronts your garden gay;
The Roman came, he bore the sway,
He bullied, bought, and sold,
Your fountain sweeps his works away
Beside your manor old!

But still his crumbling urns are found
Within the window-bay,
Where once he listened to the sound
That lulls you day by day; -
The sound of summer winds at play,
The noise of waters cold
To Yarty wandering on their way,

Beside your manor old!

The Roman fell: his firm-set bound
Became the Saxon's stay;
The bells made music all around
For monks in cloisters grey,
Till fled the monks in disarray
From their warm chantry's fold,
Old Abbots slumber as they may,
Beside your manor old!

ENVOY

Creeds, empires, peoples, all decay,
Down into darkness, rolled;
May life that's fleet be sweet, I pray,
Beside your manor old.

A DREAM IN JUNE

In twilight of the longest day
I lingered over Lucian,
Till ere the dawn a dreamy way
My spirit found, untrod of man,
Between the green sky and the grey.

Amid the soft dusk suddenly
More light than air I seemed to sail,
Afloat upon the ocean sky,

While through the faint blue, clear and pale,
I saw the mountain clouds go by:
My barque had thought for helm and sail,
And one mist wreath for canopy.

Like torches on a marble floor
Reflected, so the wild stars shone,
Within the abysmal hyaline,
Till the day widened more and more,
And sank to sunset, and was gone,
And then, as burning beacons shine
On summits of a mountain isle,
A light to folk on sea that fare,
So the sky's beacons for a while
Burned in these islands of the air.

Then from a starry island set
Where one swift tide of wind there flows,
Came scent of lily and violet,
Narcissus, hyacinth, and rose,
Laurel, and myrtle buds, and vine,
So delicate is the air and fine:
And forests of all fragrant trees
Sloped seaward from the central hill,
And ever clamorous were these

With singing of glad birds; and still
Such music came as in the woods
Most lonely, consecrate to Pan,
The Wind makes, in his many moods,
Upon the pipes some shepherd Man,
Hangs up, in thanks for victory!
On these shall mortals play no more,

But the Wind doth touch them, over and o'er,
And the Wind's breath in the reeds will sigh.

Between the daylight and the dark
That island lies in silver air,
And suddenly my magic barque
Wheeled, and ran in, and grounded there;
And by me stood the sentinel
Of them who in the island dwell;
All smiling did he bind my hands,
With rushes green and rosy bands,
They have no harsher bonds than these
The people of the pleasant lands
Within the wash of the airy seas!

Then was I to their city led:
Now all of ivory and gold
The great walls were that garlanded
The temples in their shining fold,
(Each fane of beryl built, and each
Girt with its grove of shadowy beech,)
And all about the town, and through,
There flowed a River fed with dew,
As sweet as roses, and as clear
As mountain crystals pure and cold,
And with his waves that water kissed
The gleaming altars of amethyst
That smoke with victims all the year,
And sacred are to the Gods of old.

There sat three Judges by the Gate,
And I was led before the Three,
And they but looked on me, and straight

The rosy bonds fell down from me
Who, being innocent, was free;
And I might wander at my will
About that City on the hill,
Among the happy people clad
In purple weeds of woven air
Hued like the webs that Twilight weaves
At shut of languid summer eves
So light their raiment seemed; and glad
Was every face I looked on there!

There was no heavy heat, no cold,
The dwellers there wax never old,
Nor wither with the waning time,
But each man keeps that age he had
When first he won the fairy clime.
The Night falls never from on high,
Nor ever burns the heat of noon.
But such soft light eternally
Shines, as in silver dawns of June
Before the Sun hath climbed the sky!

Within these pleasant streets and wide,
The souls of Heroes go and come,
Even they that fell on either side
Beneath the walls of Ilium;
And sunlike in that shadowy isle
The face of Helen and her smile
Makes glad the souls of them that knew
Grief for her sake a little while!
And all true Greeks and wise are there;
And with his hand upon the hair
Of Phaedo, saw I Socrates,

About him many youths and fair,
Hylas, Narcissus, and with these
Him whom the quoit of Phoebus slew
By fleet Eurotas, unaware!

All these their mirth and pleasure made
Within the plain Elysian,
The fairest meadow that may be,
With all green fragrant trees for shade
And every scented wind to fan,
And sweetest flowers to strew the lea;
The soft Winds are their servants fleet
To fetch them every fruit at will
And water from the river chill;
And every bird that singeth sweet
Throstle, and merle, and nightingale
Brings blossoms from the dewy vale, -
Lily, and rose, and asphodel -
With these doth each guest twine his crown
And wreathe his cup, and lay him down
Beside some friend he loveth well.

There with the shining Souls I lay
When, lo, a Voice that seemed to say,
In far-off haunts of Memory,
Whoso death taste the Dead Men's bread,
Shall dwell for ever with these Dead,
Nor ever shall his body lie
Beside his friends, on the grey hill
Where rains weep, and the curlews shrill
And the brown water wanders by!

Then did a new soul in me wake,

The dead men's bread I feared to break,
Their fruit I would not taste indeed
Were it but a pomegranate seed.
Nay, not with these I made my choice
To dwell for ever and rejoice,
For otherwhere the River rolls
That girds the home of Christian souls,
And these my whole heart seeks are found
On otherwise enchanted ground.

Even so I put the cup away,
The vision wavered, dimmed, and broke,
And, nowise sorrowing, I woke
While, grey among the ruins grey
Chill through the dwellings of the dead,
The Dawn crept o'er the Northern sea,
Then, in a moment, flushed to red,
Flushed all the broken minster old,
And turned the shattered stones to gold,
And wakened half the world with me!

L'ENVOI--To E. W. G.

(Who also had rhymed on the Fortune Islands of Lucian).

Each in the self-same field we glean
The field of the Samosatene,
Each something takes and something leaves
And this must choose, and that forego

In Lucian's visionary sheaves,
To twine a modern posy so;
But all any gleanings, truth to tell,
Are mixed with mournful asphodel,
While yours are wreathed with poppies red,
With flowers that Helen's feet have kissed,
With leaves of vine that garlanded
The Syrian Pantagruelist,
The sage who laughed the world away,
Who mocked at Gods, and men, and care,
More sweet of voice than Rabelais,
And lighter-hearted than Voltaire.

A VISION IN THE STRAND

The jaded light of late July
Shone yellow down the dusty Strand,
The anxious people bustled by,
Policeman, Pressman, you and I,
And thieves, and judges of the land.

So swift they strode they had not time
To mark the humours of the Town,
But I, that mused an idle rhyme,
Looked here and there, and up and down,
And many a rapid cart I spied
That drew, as fast as ponies can,
The Newspapers of either side,
These joys of every Englishman!

The Standard here, the Echo there,
And cultured ev'ning papers fair,
With din and fuss and shout and blare
Through all the eager land they bare,
The rumours of our little span.

'Midst these, but ah, more slow of speed,
A biggish box of sanguine hue
Was tugged on a velocipede,
And in and out the crowd, and through,
An earnest stripling urged it well
Perched on a cranky tricycle!

A seedy tricycle he rode,
Perchance some three miles in the hour,
But, on the big red box that glowed
Behind him, was a name of Power,
JUSTICE, (I read it e'er I wist,)
THE ORGAN OF THE SOCIALIST!

The paper carts fled fleetly by
And vanished up the roaring Strand,
And eager purchasers drew nigh
Each with his penny in his hand,
But JUSTICE, scarce more fleet than I,
Began to permeate the land,
And dark, methinks, the twilight fell,
Or ever JUSTICE reached Pall Mall.

Oh Man, (I stopped to moralize,)
How eager thou to fight with Fate,
To bring Astraea from the skies;

Yet ah, how too inadequate
The means by which thou fain wouldst cope
With Laws and Morals, King and Pope!
"JUSTICE!"--how prompt the witling's sneer, -
"Justice! Thou wouldst have Justice here!
And each poor man should be a squire,
Each with his competence a year,
Each with sufficient beef and beer,
And all things matched to his desire,
While all the Middle Classes should
With every vile Capitalist
Be clean reformed away for good,
And vanish like a morning mist!

"Ah splendid Vision, golden time,
An end of hunger, cold, and crime.
An end of Rent, an end of Rank,
An end of balance at the Bank,
An end of everything that's meant
To bring Investors five per cent!"

How fair doth Justice seem, I cried,
Yet oh, how strong the embattled powers
That war against on every side
Justice, and this great dream of ours,
And what have we to plead our cause
'Gainst Masters, Capital, and laws,
What but a big red box indeed,
With copies of a weekly screed,
That's slowly jolted, up and down,
Behind an old velocipede
To clamour JUSTICE through the town:
How touchingly inadequate

These arms wherewith we'd vanquish Fate!

Nay, the old Order shall endure
And little change the years shall know,
And still the Many shall be poor,
And still the Poor shall dwell in woe;
Firm in the iron Law of things
The strong shall be the wealthy still,
And (called Capitalists or Kings)
Shall seize and hoard the fruits of skill.
Leaving the weaker for their gain,
Leaving the gentler for their prize
Such dens and husks as beasts disdain, -
Till slowly from the wrinkled skies
The fireless frozen Sun shall wane,
Nor Summer come with golden grain;
Till men be glad, mid frost and snow
To live such equal lives of pain
As now the hutted Eskimo!
Then none shall plough nor garner seed,
Then, on some last sad human shore,
Equality shall reign indeed,
The Rich shall be with us no more,
Thus, and not otherwise, shall come
The new, the true Millennium!

ALMAE MATRES--(ST. ANDREWS, 1862. OXFORD, 1865)

St. Andrews by the Northern sea,
A haunted town it is to me!
A little city, worn and grey,
The grey North Ocean girds it round.
And o'er the rocks, and up the bay,
The long sea-rollers surge and sound.
And still the thin and biting spray
Drives down the melancholy street,
And still endure, and still decay,
Towers that the salt winds vainly beat.
Ghost-like and shadowy they stand
Dim mirrored in the wet sea-sand.

St. Leonard's chapel, long ago
We loitered idly where the tall
Fresh budded mountain ashes blow
Within thy desecrated wall:
The tough roots rent the tomb below,
The April birds sang clamorous,
We did not dream, we could not know
How hardly Fate would deal with us!

O, broken minster, looking forth
Beyond the bay, above the town,
O, winter of the kindly North,
O, college of the scarlet gown,

And shining sands beside the sea,
And stretch of links beyond the sand,
Once more I watch you, and to me
It is as if I touched his hand!

And therefore art thou yet more dear,
O, little city, grey and sere,
Though shrunken from thine ancient pride
And lonely by thy lonely sea,
Than these fair halls on Isis' side,
Where Youth an hour came back to me!

A land of waters green and clear,
Of willows and of poplars tall,
And, in the spring time of the year,
The white may breaking over all,
And Pleasure quick to come at call.
And summer rides by marsh and wold,
And Autumn with her crimson pall
About the towers of Magdalen rolled;
And strange enchantments from the past,
And memories of the friends of old,
And strong Tradition, binding fast
The "flying terms" with bands of gold, -

All these hath Oxford: all are dear,
But dearer far the little town,
The drifting surf, the wintry year,
The college of the scarlet gown,
St. Andrews by the Northern sea,
That is a haunted town to me!

DESIDERIUM--IN MEMORIAM S. F. A.

The call of homing rooks, the shrill
Song of some bird that watches late,
The cries of children break the still
Sad twilight by the churchyard gate.

And o'er your far-off tomb the grey
Sad twilight broods, and from the trees
The rooks call on their homeward way,
And are you heedless quite of these?

The clustered rowan berries red
And Autumn's may, the clematis,
They droop above your dreaming head,
And these, and all things must you miss?

Ah, you that loved the twilight air,
The dim lit hour of quiet best,
At last, at last you have your share
Of what life gave so seldom, rest!

Yes, rest beyond all dreaming deep,
Or labour, nearer the Divine,
And pure from fret, and smooth as sleep,
And gentle as thy soul, is thine!

So let it be! But could I know
That thou in this soft autumn eve,
This hush of earth that pleased thee so,

Hadst pleasure still, I might not grieve.

BALLADE OF MIDDLE AGE

Our youth began with tears and sighs,
With seeking what we could not find;
Our verses all were threnodies,
In elegiacs still we whined;
Our ears were deaf, our eyes were blind,
We sought and knew not what we sought.
We marvel, now we look behind:
Life's more amusing than we thought!

Oh, foolish youth, untimely wise!
Oh, phantoms of the sickly mind!
What? not content with seas and skies,
With rainy clouds and southern wind,
With common cares and faces kind,
With pains and joys each morning brought?
Ah, old, and worn, and tired we find
Life's more amusing than we thought!

Though youth "turns spectre-thin and dies,"
To mourn for youth we're not inclined;
We set our souls on salmon flies,
We whistle where we once repined.
Confound the woes of human-kind!
By Heaven we're "well deceived," I wot;
Who hum, contented or resigned,

"Life's more amusing than we thought!"

ENVOY

O nate mecum, worn and lined
Our faces show, but THAT is naught;
Our hearts are young 'neath wrinkled rind:
Life's more amusing than we thought!

THE LAST CAST--THE ANGLER'S APOLOGY

Just one cast more! how many a year
Beside how many a pool and stream,
Beneath the falling leaves and sere,
I've sighed, reeled up, and dreamed my dream!

Dreamed of the sport since April first
Her hands fulfilled of flowers and snow,
Adown the pastoral valleys burst
Where Ettrick and where Teviot flow.

Dreamed of the singing showers that break,
And sting the lochs, or near or far,
And rouse the trout, and stir "the take"
From Urigil to Lochinvar.

Dreamed of the kind propitious sky

O'er Ari Innes brooding grey;
The sea trout, rushing at the fly,
Breaks the black wave with sudden spray!

* * *

Brief are man's days at best; perchance
I waste my own, who have not seen
The castled palaces of France
Shine on the Loire in summer green.

And clear and fleet Eurotas still,
You tell me, laves his reedy shore,
And flows beneath his fabled hill
Where Dian drave the chase of yore.

And "like a horse unbroken" yet
The yellow stream with rush and foam,
'Neath tower, and bridge, and parapet,
Girdles his ancient mistress, Rome!

I may not see them, but I doubt
If seen I'd find them half so fair
As ripples of the rising trout
That feed beneath the elms of Yair.

Nay, Spring I'd meet by Tweed or Ail,
And Summer by Loch Assynt's deep,
And Autumn in that lonely vale
Where wedded Avons westward sweep,

Or where, amid the empty fields,
Among the bracken of the glen,

Her yellow wreath October yields,
To crown the crystal brows of Ken.

Unseen, Eurotas, southward steal,
Unknown, Alpheus, westward glide,
You never heard the ringing reel,
The music of the water side!

Though Gods have walked your woods among,
Though nymphs have fled your banks along;
You speak not that familiar tongue
Tweed murmurs like my cradle song.

My cradle song,--nor other hymn
I'd choose, nor gentler requiem dear
Than Tweed's, that through death's twilight dim,
Mourned in the latest Minstrel's ear!

TWILIGHT--SONNET (AFTER RICHEPIN)

Light has flown!
Through the grey
The wind's way
The sea's moan
Sound alone!
For the day
These repay
And atone!

Scarce I know,
Listening so
To the streams
Of the sea,
If old dreams
Sing to me!

BALLADE OF SUMMER--TO C. H. ARKCOLL

When strawberry pottles are common and cheap,
Ere elms be black, or limes be sere,
When midnight dances are murdering sleep,
Then comes in the sweet o' the year!
And far from Fleet Street, far from here,
The Summer is Queen in the length of the land,
And moonlit nights they are soft and clear,
When fans for a penny are sold in the Strand!

When clamour that doves in the lindens keep
Mingles with musical plash of the weir,
Where drowned green tresses of crowsfoot creep,
Then comes in the sweet o' the year!
And better a crust and a beaker of beer,
With rose-hung hedges on either hand,
Than a palace in town and a prince's cheer,
When fans for a penny are sold in the Strand!

When big trout late in the twilight leap,
When cuckoo clamoureth far and near,

When glittering scythes in the hayfield reap,
Then comes in the sweet o' the year!
And it's oh to sail, with the wind to steer,
Where kine knee deep in the water stand,
On a Highland loch, on a Lowland mere,
When fans for a penny are sold in the Strand!

ENVOY.

Friend, with the fops while we dawdle here,
Then comes in the sweet o' the year!
And the Summer runs out, like grains of sand,
When fans for a penny are sold in the Strand!

BALLADE OF CHRISTMAS GHOSTS

Between the moonlight and the fire
In winter twilights long ago,
What ghosts we raised for your desire
To make your merry blood run slow!
How old, how grave, how wise we grow!
No Christmas ghost can make us chill,
Save THOSE that troop in mournful row,
The ghosts we all can raise at will!

The beasts can talk in barn and byre
On Christmas Eve, old legends know,
As year by year the years retire,
We men fall silent then I trow,

Such sights hath Memory to show,
Such voices from the silence thrill,
Such shapes return with Christmas snow, -
The ghosts we all can raise at will.

Oh, children of the village choir,
Your carols on the midnight throw,
Oh bright across the mist and mire
Ye ruddy hearths of Christmas glow!
Beat back the dread, beat down the woe,
Let's cheerily descend the hill;
Be welcome all, to come or go,
The ghosts we all can raise at will!

ENVOY.

Friend, sursum corda, soon or slow
We part, like guests who've joyed their fill;
Forget them not, nor mourn them so,
The ghosts we all can raise at will!

LOVE'S EASTER--SONNET

Love died here
Long ago; -
O'er his bier,
Lying low,
Poppies throw;
Shed no tear;

Year by year,
Roses blow!

Year by year,
Adon--dear
To Love's Queen -
Does not die!
Wakes when green
May is nigh!

BALLADE OF THE GIRTON GIRL

She has just "put her gown on" at Girton,
She is learned in Latin and Greek,
But lawn tennis she plays with a skirt on
That the prudish remark with a shriek.
In her accents, perhaps, she is weak
(Ladies ARE, one observes with a sigh),
But in Algebra--THERE she's unique,
But her forte's to evaluate pi.

She can talk about putting a "spirt on"
(I admit, an unmaidenly freak),
And she dearly delighteth to flirt on
A punt in some shadowy creek;
Should her bark, by mischance, spring a leak,
She can swim as a swallow can fly;
She can fence, she can put with a cleek,
But her forte's to evaluate pi.

She has lectured on Scopas and Myrton,
Coins, vases, mosaics, the antique,
Old tiles with the secular dirt on,
Old marbles with noses to seek.
And her Cobet she quotes by the week,
And she's written on [Greek text: kev] and on [Greek text: kai],
And her service is swift and oblique,
But her forte's to evaluate pi.

ENVOY.

Princess, like a rose is her cheek,
And her eyes are as blue as the sky,
And I'd speak, had I courage to speak,
But--her forte's to evaluate pi.

RONSARD'S GRAVE

Ye wells, ye founts that fall
From the steep mountain wall,
That fall, and flash, and fleet
With silver feet,

Ye woods, ye streams that lave
The meadows with your wave,
Ye hills, and valley fair,
Attend my prayer!

When Heaven and Fate decree
My latest hour for me,
When I must pass away
From pleasant day,

I ask that none my break
The marble for my sake,
Wishful to make more fair
My sepulchre.

Only a laurel tree
Shall shade the grave of me,
Only Apollo's bough
Shall guard me now!

Now shall I be at rest
Among the spirits blest,
The happy dead that dwell -
Where,--who may tell?

The snow and wind and hail
May never there prevail,
Nor ever thunder fall
Nor storm at all.

But always fadeless there
The woods are green and fair,
And faithful ever more
Spring to that shore!

There shall I ever hear
Alcaeus' music clear,
And sweetest of all things

There SAPPHO sings.

SAN TERENZO

(The village in the bay of Spezia, near which Shelley was living before the wreck of the Don Juan.)

Mid April seemed like some November day,
When through the glassy waters, dull as lead,
Our boat, like shadowy barques that bear the dead,
Slipped down the long shores of the Spezian bay,
Rounded a point,--and San Terenzo lay
Before us, that gay village, yellow and red,
The roof that covered Shelley's homeless head, -
His house, a place deserted, bleak and grey.

The waves broke on the door-step; fishermen
Cast their long nets, and drew, and cast again.
Deep in the ilex woods we wandered free,
When suddenly the forest glades were stirred
With waving pinions, and a great sea bird
Flew forth, like Shelley's spirit, to the sea!

1880

ROMANCE

My Love dwelt in a Northern land.
A grey tower in a forest green
Was hers, and far on either hand
The long wash of the waves was seen,
And leagues on leagues of yellow sand,
The woven forest boughs between!

And through the silver Northern night
The sunset slowly died away,
And herds of strange deer, lily-white,
Stole forth among the branches grey;
About the coming of the light,
They fled like ghosts before the day!

I know not if the forest green
Still girdles round that castle grey;
I know not if the boughs between
The white deer vanish ere the day;
Above my Love the grass is green,
My heart is colder than the clay!

BALLADE OF HIS OWN COUNTRY

I scribbled on a fly-book's leaves
Among the shining salmon-flies;
A song for summer-time that grieves
I scribbled on a fly-book's leaves.
Between grey sea and golden sheaves,
Beneath the soft wet Morvern skies,
I scribbled on a fly-book's leaves
Among the shining salmon-flies.

TO C. H. ARKCOLL

Let them boast of Arabia, oppressed
By the odour of myrrh on the breeze;
In the isles of the East and the West
That are sweet with the cinnamon trees
Let the sandal-wood perfume the seas;
Give the roses to Rhodes and to Crete,
We are more than content, if you please,
With the smell of bog-myrtle and peat!

Though Dan Virgil enjoyed himself best
With the scent of the limes, when the bees
Hummed low 'round the doves in their nest,
While the vintagers lay at their ease,

Had he sung in our northern degrees,
He'd have sought a securer retreat,
He'd have dwelt, where the heart of us flees,
With the smell of bog-myrtle and peat!

Oh, the broom has a chivalrous crest
And the daffodil's fair on the leas,
And the soul of the Southron might rest,
And be perfectly happy with these;
But WE, that were nursed on the knees
Of the hills of the North, we would fleet
Where our hearts might their longing appease
With the smell of bog-myrtle and peat!

ENVOY

Ah Constance, the land of our quest
It is far from the sounds of the street,
Where the Kingdom of Galloway's blest
With the smell of bog-myrtle and peat!

VILLANELLE--(To M. Joseph Boulmier, author of "Les Villanelles.")

Villanelle, why art thou mute?
Hath the singer ceased to sing?
Hath the Master lost his lute?

Many a pipe and scrannel flute
On the breeze their discords fling;
Villanelle, why art THOU mute?

Sound of tumult and dispute,
Noise of war the echoes bring;
Hath the Master lost his lute?

Once he sang of bud and shoot
In the season of the Spring;
Villanelle, why art thou mute?

Fading leaf and falling fruit
Say, "The year is on the wing,
Hath the Master lost his lute?"

Ere the axe lie at the root,
Ere the winter come as king,
Villanelle, why art thou mute?
Hath the Master lost his lute?

TRIOLETS AFTER MOSCHUS

[Paragraph of Greek text]

Alas, for us no second spring,
Like mallows in the garden-bed,
For these the grave has lost his sting,
Alas, for US no second spring,

Who sleep without awakening,
And, dead, for ever more are dead,
Alas, for us no second spring,
Like mallows in the garden-bed!

Alas, the strong, the wise, the brave
That boast themselves the sons of men!
Once they go down into the grave -
Alas, the strong, the wise, the brave, -
They perish and have none to save,
They are sown, and are not raised again;
Alas, the strong, the wise, the brave,
That boast themselves the sons of men!

BALLADE OF CRICKET--TO T. W. LANG

The burden of hard hitting: slog away!
Here shalt thou make a "five" and there a "four,"
And then upon thy bat shalt lean, and say,
That thou art in for an uncommon score.
Yea, the loud ring applauding thee shall roar,
And thou to rival THORNTON shalt aspire,
When lo, the Umpire gives thee "leg before," -
"This is the end of every man's desire!"

The burden of much bowling, when the stay
Of all thy team is "collared," swift or slower,
When "bailers" break not in their wonted way,
And "yorkers" come not off as here-to-fore,

When length balls shoot no more, ah never more,
When all deliveries lose their former fire,
When bats seem broader than the broad barn-door, -
"This is the end of every man's desire!"

The burden of long fielding, when the clay
Clings to thy shoon in sudden shower's downpour,
And running still thou stumblest, or the ray
Of blazing suns doth bite and burn thee sore,
And blind thee till, forgetful of thy lore,
Thou dost most mournfully misjudge a "skyer,"
And lose a match the Fates cannot restore, -
"This is the end of every man's desire!"

ENVOY.

Alas, yet liefer on Youth's hither shore
Would I be some poor Player on scant hire,
Than King among the old, who play no more, -
"THIS is the end of every man's desire!"

THE LAST MAYING

"It is told of the last Lovers which watched May-night in the forest, before men brought the tidings of the Gospel to this land, that they beheld no Fairies, nor Dwarfs, nor no such Thing, but the very Venus herself, who bade them 'make such cheer as they might, for' said she, 'I shall live no more in these Woods, nor shall ye endure to see another May time.'"--EDMUND GORLIOT, "Of

Phantasies and Omens," p. 149. (1573.)

"Whence do ye come, with the dew on your hair?
From what far land are the boughs ye bear,
The blossoms and buds upon breasts and tresses,
The light burned white in your faces fair?"

"In a falling fane have we built our house,
With the dying Gods we have held carouse,
And our lips are wan from their wild caresses,
Our hands are filled with their holy boughs.

As we crossed the lawn in the dying day
No fairy led us to meet the May,
But the very Goddess loved by lovers,
In mourning raiment of green and grey.

She was not decked as for glee and game,
She was not veiled with the veil of flame,
The saffron veil of the Bride that covers
The face that is flushed with her joy and shame.

On the laden branches the scent and dew
Mingled and met, and as snow to strew
The woodland rides and the fragrant grasses,
White flowers fell as the night wind blew.

Tears and kisses on lips and eyes
Mingled and met amid laughter and sighs
For grief that abides, and joy that passes,
For pain that tarries and mirth that flies.

It chanced as the dawning grew to grey

Pale and sad on our homeward way,
With weary lips, and palled with pleasure
The Goddess met us, farewell to say.

"Ye have made your choice, and the better part,
Ye chose" she said, "and the wiser art;
In the wild May night drank all the measure,
The perfect pleasure of heart and heart.

"Ye shall walk no more with the May," she said,
"Shall your love endure though the Gods be dead?
Shall the flitting flocks, mine own, my chosen,
Sing as of old, and be happy and wed?

"Yea, they are glad as of old; but you,
Fair and fleet as the dawn or the dew,
Abide no more, for the springs are frozen,
And fled the Gods that ye loved and knew.

Ye shall never know Summer again like this;
Ye shall play no more with the Fauns, I wis,
No more in the nymphs' and dryads' playtime
Shall echo and answer kiss and kiss.

"Though the flowers in your golden hair be bright,
Your golden hair shall be waste and white
On faded brows ere another May time
Bring the spring, but no more delight."

HOMERIC UNITY

The sacred keep of Ilion is rent
By shaft and pit; foiled waters wander slow
Through plains where Simois and Scamander went
To war with Gods and heroes long ago.
Not yet to tired Cassandra, lying low
In rich Mycenae, do the Fates relent:
The bones of Agamemnon are a show,
And ruined is his royal monument.

The dust and awful treasures of the Dead,
Hath Learning scattered wide, but vainly thee,
Homer, she meteth with her tool of lead,
And strives to rend thy songs; too blind to see
The crown that burns on thine immortal head
Of indivisible supremacy!

IN TINTAGEL

LUI.

Ah lady, lady, leave the creeping mist,
And leave the iron castle by the sea!

ELLE.

Nay, from the sea there came a ghost that kissed
My lips, and so I cannot come to thee!

LUI.

Ah lady, leave the cruel landward wind
That crusts the blighted flowers with bitter foam!

ELLE.

Nay, for his arms are cold and strong to bind,
And I must dwell with him and make my home!

LUI.

Come, for the Spring is fair in Joyous Guard
And down deep alleys sweet birds sing again.

ELLE.

But I must tarry with the winter hard,
And with the bitter memory of pain,
Although the Spring be fair in Joyous Guard,
And in the gardens glad birds sing again!

PISIDICE

The incident is from the Love Stories of Parthenius, who preserved fragments of a lost epic on the expedition of Achilles against Lesbos, an island allied with Troy.

The daughter of the Lesbian king
Within her bower she watched the war,
Far off she heard the arrows ring,
The smitten harness ring afar;
And, fighting from the foremost car,
Saw one that smote where all must flee;
More fair than the Immortals are
He seemed to fair Pisidice!

She saw, she loved him, and her heart
Before Achilles, Peleus' son,
Threw all its guarded gates apart,
A maiden fortress lightly won!
And, ere that day of fight was done,
No more of land or faith recked she,
But joyed in her new life begun, -
Her life of love, Pisidice!

She took a gift into her hand,
As one that had a boon to crave;
She stole across the ruined land
Where lay the dead without a grave,
And to Achilles' hand she gave

Her gift, the secret postern's key.
"To-morrow let me be thy slave!"
Moaned to her love Pisidice.

Ere dawn the Argives' clarion call
Rang down Methymna's burning street;
They slew the sleeping warriors all,
They drove the women to the fleet,
Save one, that to Achilles' feet
Clung, but, in sudden wrath, cried he:
"For her no doom but death is meet,"
And there men stoned Pisidice.

In havens of that haunted coast,
Amid the myrtles of the shore,
The moon sees many a maiden ghost
Love's outcast now and evermore.
The silence hears the shades deplore
Their hour of dear-bought love; but THEE
The waves lull, 'neath thine olives hoar,
To dreamless rest, Pisidice!

FROM THE EAST TO THE WEST

Returning from what other seas
Dost thou renew thy murmuring,
Weak Tide, and hast thou aught of these
To tell, the shores where float and cling
My love, my hope, my memories?

Say does my lady wake to note
The gold light into silver die?
Or do thy waves make lullaby,
While dreams of hers, like angels, float
Through star-sown spaces of the sky?

Ah, would such angels came to me
That dreams of mine might speak with hers,
Nor wake the slumber of the sea
With words as low as winds that be
Awake among the gossamers!

LOVE THE VAMPIRE [Greek text]

The level sands and grey,
Stretch leagues and leagues away,
Down to the border line of sky and foam,
A spark of sunset burns,
The grey tide-water turns,
Back, like a ghost from her forbidden home!

Here, without pyre or bier,
Light Love was buried here,
Alas, his grave was wide and deep enough,
Thrice, with averted head,
We cast dust on the dead,
And left him to his rest. An end of Love.

"No stone to roll away,
No seal of snow or clay,
Only soft dust above his wearied eyes,
But though the sudden sound
Of Doom should shake the ground,
And graves give up their ghosts, he will not rise!"

So each to each we said!
Ah, but to either bed
Set far apart in lands of North and South,
Love as a Vampire came
With haggard eyes aflame,
And kissed us with the kisses of his mouth!

Thenceforth in dreams must we
Each other's shadow see
Wand'ring unsatisfied in empty lands,
Still the desired face
Fleets from the vain embrace,
And still the shape evades the longing hands.

BALLADE OF THE BOOK-MAN'S PARADISE

There IS a Heaven, or here, or there, -
A Heaven there is, for me and you,
Where bargains meet for purses spare,
Like ours, are not so far and few.
Thuanus' bees go humming through
The learned groves, 'neath rainless skies,

O'er volumes old and volumes new,
Within that Book-man's Paradise!

There treasures bound for Longepierre
Keep brilliant their morocco blue,
There Hookes' AMANDA is not rare,
Nor early tracts upon Peru!
Racine is common as Rotrou,
No Shakespeare Quarto search defies,
And Caxtons grow as blossoms grew,
Within that Book-man's Paradise!

There's Eve,--not our first mother fair, -
But Clovis Eve, a binder true;
Thither does Bauzonnet repair,
Derome, Le Gascon, Padeloup!
But never come the cropping crew
That dock a volume's honest size,
Nor they that "letter" backs askew,
Within that Book-man's Paradise!

ENVOY

Friend, do not Heber and De Thou,
And Scott, and Southey, kind and wise,
La chasse au bouquin still pursue
Within that Book-man's Paradise?

BALLADE OF A FRIAR

(Clement Marot's Frere Lubin, though translated by Longfellow and others, has not hitherto been rendered into the original measure, of ballade e double refrain.)

Some ten or twenty times a day,
To bustle to the town with speed,
To dabble in what dirt he may, -
Le Frere Lubin's the man you need!
But any sober life to lead
Upon an exemplary plan,
Requires a Christian indeed, -
Le Frere Lubin is NOT the man!

Another's wealth on his to lay,
With all the craft of guile and greed,
To leave you bare of pence or pay, -
Le Frere Lubin's the man you need!
But watch him with the closest heed,
And dun him with what force you can, -
He'll not refund, howe'er you plead, -
Le Frere Lubin is NOT the man!

An honest girl to lead astray,
With subtle saw and promised meed,
Requires no cunning crone and grey, -
Le Frere Lubin's the man you need!
He preaches an ascetic creed,
But,--try him with the water can -

A dog will drink, whate'er his breed, -
Le Frere Lubin is NOT the man!

ENVOY

In good to fail, in ill succeed,
Le Frere Lubin's the man you need!
In honest works to lead the van,
Le Frere Lubin is NOT the man!

BALLADE OF NEGLECTED MERIT {1}

I have scribbled in verse and in prose,
I have painted "arrangements in greens,"
And my name is familiar to those
Who take in the high class magazines;
I compose; I've invented machines;
I have written an "Essay on Rhyme";
For my county I played, in my teens,
But--I am not in "Men of the Time!"

I have lived, as a chief, with the Crows;
I have "interviewed" Princes and Queens;
I have climbed the Caucasian snows;
I abstain, like the ancients, from beans, -
I've a guess what Pythagoras means,
When he says that to eat them's a crime, -
I have lectured upon the Essenes,
But--I am not in "Men of the Time!"

I've a fancy as morbid as Poe's,
I can tell what is meant by "Shebeens,"
I have breasted the river that flows
Through the land of the wild Gadarenes;
I can gossip with Burton on skenes,
I can imitate Irving (the Mime),
And my sketches are quainter than Keene's,
But--I am not in "Men of the Time!"

ENVOY

So the tower of mine eminence leans
Like the Pisan, and mud is its lime;
I'm acquainted with Dukes and with Deans,
But--I am not in "Men of the Time!"

BALLADE OF RAILWAY NOVELS

Let others praise analysis
And revel in a "cultured" style,
And follow the subjective Miss {2}
From Boston to the banks of Nile,
Rejoice in anti-British bile,
And weep for fickle hero's woe,
These twain have shortened many a mile,
Miss Braddon and Gaboriau.

These damsels of "Democracy's,"

How long they stop at every stile!
They smile, and we are told, I wis,
Ten subtle reasons WHY they smile.
Give ME your villains deeply vile,
Give me Lecoq, Jottrat, and Co.,
Great artists of the ruse and wile,
Miss Braddon and Gaboriau!

Oh, novel readers, tell me this,
Can prose that's polished by the file,
Like great Boisgobey's mysteries,
Wet days and weary ways beguile,
And man to living reconcile,
Like these whose every trick we know?
The agony how high they pile,
Miss Braddon and Gaboriau!

ENVOY

Ah, friend, how many and many a while
They've made the slow time fleetly flow,
And solaced pain and charmed exile,
Miss Braddon and Gaboriau.

THE CLOUD CHORUS (FROM ARISTOPHANES)

Socrates speaks.

Hither, come hither, ye Clouds renowned, and unveil yourselves

here;
Come, though ye dwell on the sacred crests of Olympian snow,
Or whether ye dance with the Nereid choir in the gardens clear,
Or whether your golden urns are dipped in Nile's overflow,
Or whether you dwell by Maeotis mere
Or the snows of Mimas, arise! appear!
And hearken to us, and accept our gifts ere ye rise and go.

The Clouds sing.

Immortal Clouds from the echoing shore
Of the father of streams, from the sounding sea,
Dewy and fleet, let us rise and soar.
Dewy and gleaming, and fleet are we!
Let us look on the tree-clad mountain crest,
On the sacred earth where the fruits rejoice,
On the waters that murmur east and west
On the tumbling sea with his moaning voice,
For unwearied glitters the Eye of the Air,
And the bright rays gleam;
Then cast we our shadows of mist, and fare
In our deathless shapes to glance everywhere
From the height of the heaven, on the land and air,
And the Ocean stream.

Let us on, ye Maidens that bring the Rain,
Let us gaze on Pallas' citadel,
In the country of Cecrops, fair and dear
The mystic land of the holy cell,
Where the Rites unspoken securely dwell,
And the gifts of the Gods that know not stain
And a people of mortals that know not fear.
For the temples tall, and the statues fair,

And the feasts of the Gods are holiest there,
The feasts of Immortals, the chaplets of flowers
And the Bromian mirth at the coming of spring,
And the musical voices that fill the hours,
And the dancing feet of the Maids that sing!

BALLADE OF LITERARY FAME

"All these for Fourpence."

Oh, where are the endless Romances
Our grandmothers used to adore?
The Knights with their helms and their lances,
Their shields and the favours they wore?
And the Monks with their magical lore?
They have passed to Oblivion and Nox,
They have fled to the shadowy shore, -
They are all in the Fourpenny Box!

And where the poetical fancies
Our fathers rejoiced in, of yore?
The lyric's melodious expanses,
The Epics in cantos a score?
They have been and are not: no more
Shall the shepherds drive silvery flocks,
Nor the ladies their languors deplore, -
They are all in the Fourpenny Box!

And the Music! The songs and the dances?

The tunes that Time may not restore?
And the tomes where Divinity prances?
And the pamphlets where Heretics roar?
They have ceased to be even a bore, -
The Divine, and the Sceptic who mocks, -
They are "cropped," they are "foxed" to the core, -
They are all in the Fourpenny Box!

ENVOY

Suns beat on them; tempests downpour,
On the chest without cover or locks,
Where they lie by the Bookseller's door, -
They are ALL in the Fourpenny Box!

[Greek title]

I would my days had been in other times,
A moment in the long unnumbered years
That knew the sway of Horus and of hawk,
In peaceful lands that border on the Nile.

I would my days had been in other times,
Lulled by the sacrifice and mumbled hymn
Between the Five great Rivers, or in shade
And shelter of the cool Himalayan hills.

I would my days had been in other times,
That I in some old abbey of Touraine

Had watched the rounding grapes, and lived my life,
Ere ever Luther came or Rabelais!

I would my days had been in other times,
When quiet life to death not terrible
Drifted, as ashes of the Santhal dead
Drift down the sacred Rivers to the Sea!

A VERY WOFUL BALLADE OF THE ART CRITIC
(TO E. A. ABBEY.)

A spirit came to my sad bed,
And weary sad that night was I,
Who'd tottered, since the dawn was red,
Through miles of Grosvenor Gallery,
Yea, leagues of long Academy
Awaited me when morn grew white,
'Twas then the Spirit whispered nigh,
"Take up the pen, my friend, and write!

"Of many a portrait grey as lead,
Of many a mustard-coloured sky,
Say much, where little should be said,
Lay on thy censure dexterously,
With microscopic glances pry
At textures, Tadema's delight,
Praise foreign swells they always sky,
Take up the pen, my friend, and write!"

I answered, "'Tis for daily bread,
A sorry crust, I ween, and dry,
That still, with aching feet and head,
I push this lawful industry,
'Mid pictures hung or low, or high,
But, touching that which I indite,
Do artists hold me lovingly?
Take up the pen, my friend, and write."

[The Spirit writeth in form of]

ENVOY

"They fain would black thy dexter eye,
They hate thee with a bitter spite,
But scribble since thou must, or die,
Take tip the pen, my friend, and write!"

ART'S MARTYR

Telleth of a young man that fain would be fairly tattooed on his flesh, after the heathen manner, in devices of blue, and that, falling among the Dyacks, a folk of Borneo, was by them tattooed in modern fashion and device, and of his misery that fell upon him, and his outlawry.

He said, The China on the shelf
Is very fair to view,

And wherefore should mine outer self,
Not correspond thereto?
In blue
My frame I must tattoo.

Where may tattooing men abound,
And ah, where might they be?
Nay, well I wot they are not found
In lands of Christentie,
(Quoth he)
But I must cross the sea!

So forth he sailed to Borneo,
(A land that culture lacks,)
And there his money did bestow
To purchase pricks and hacks,
(Dyacks
Are famed tattooing blacks.)

But European commerce had
Debased the savage kind,
And they this most unhappy lad
Before (and eke behind)
Designed
In colours to their mind!

Such awful colours as are blent
On terrible placards
Where flames the fierce advertisement
Yea, or on Christmas cards
(Not Ward's,
But common Christmas cards!)

Thus never more to Chelsea might
The luckless boy return,
He knew himself too dreadful, quite,
A thing his friends would spurn,
And turn
To praise some Grecian urn!

But still he dwells in Borneo,
A land that culture lacks,
And there they all admire him so,
They bring him heads in sacks,
Dyacks
Are NOT aesthetic blacks!

THE PALACE O BRIC-A-BRAC

Here, where old Nankin glitters,
Here, where men's tumult seems
As faint as feeble twitters
Of sparrows heard in dreams,
We watch Limoges enamel,
An old chased silver camel,
A shawl, the gift of Schamyl,
And manuscripts in reams.

Here, where the hawthorn pattern
On flawless cup and plate
Need fear no housemaid slattern,
Fell minister of fate,

'Mid webs divinely woven,
And helms and hauberks cloven,
On music of Beethoven
We dream and meditate.

We know not, and we need not
To know how mortals fare,
Of Bills that pass, or speed not,
Time finds us unaware,
Yea, creeds and codes may crumble,
And Dilke and Gladstone stumble,
And eat the pie that's humble,
We neither know nor care!

Can kings or clergies alter
The crackle on one plate?
Can creeds or systems palter
With what is truly great?
With Corots and with Millets,
With April daffodillies,
Or make the maiden lilies
Bloom early or bloom late?

Nay, here 'midst Rhodian roses,
'Midst tissues of Cashmere,
The Soul sublime reposes,
And knows not hope nor fear;
Here all she sees her own is,
And musical her moan is,
O'er Caxtons and Bodonis,
Aldine and Elzevir!

RONDEAUX OF THE GALLERIES

Camelot

In Camelot how grey and green
The Damsels dwell, how sad their teen,
In Camelot how green and grey
The melancholy poplars sway.
I wis I wot not what they mean
Or wherefore, passionate and lean,
The maidens mope their loves between,
Not seeming to have much to say,
In Camelot.
Yet there hath armour goodly sheen
The blossoms in the apple treen,
(To spell the Camelotian way)
Show fragrant through the doubtful day,
And Master's work is often seen
In Camelot!

Philistia

Philistia! Maids in muslin white
With flannelled oarsmen oft delight
To drift upon thy streams, and float
In Salter's most luxurious boat;
In buff and boots the cheery knight
Returns (quite safe) from Naseby fight;
Thy humblest folk are clean and bright,
Thou still must win the public vote,

Philistia!
Observe the High Church curate's coat,
The realistic hansom note!
Ah, happy land untouched of blight,
Smirks, Bishops, Babies, left and right,
We know thine every charm by rote,
Philistia!

THE BARBAROUS BIRD-GODS: A SAVAGE PARABASIS

In the Aves of Aristophanes, the Bird Chorus declare that they are older than the Gods, and greater benefactors of men. This idea recurs in almost all savage mythologies, and I have made the savage Bird-gods state their own case.

The Birds sing:

We would have you to wit, that on eggs though we sit, and are spiked on the spit, and are baked in the pan,
Birds are older by far than your ancestors are, and made love and made war ere the making of Man!
For when all things were dark, not a glimmer nor spark, and the world like a barque without rudder or sail
Floated on through the night, 'twas a Bird struck a light, 'twas a flash from the bright feather'd Tonatiu's {3} tail!
Then the Hawk {4} with some dry wood flew up in the sky, and afar, safe and high, the Hawk lit Sun and Moon,

Rhymes a la Mode

And the Birds of the air they rejoiced everywhere, and they recked not of care that should come on them soon.
For the Hawk, so they tell, was then known as Pundjel, {5} and a-musing he fell at the close of the day;
Then he went on the quest, as we thought, of a nest, with some bark of the best, and a clawful of clay. {6}
And with these did he frame two birds lacking a name, without feathers (his game was a puzzle to all);
Next around them he fluttered a-dancing, and muttered; and, lastly, he uttered a magical call:
Then the figures of clay, as they featherless lay, they leaped up, who but they, and embracing they fell,
And THIS was the baking of Man, and his making; but now he's forsaking his Father, Pundjel!
Now these creatures of mire, they kept whining for fire, and to crown their desire who was found but the Wren?
To the high heaven he came, from the Sun stole he flame, and for this has a name in the memory of men! {7}
And in India who for the Soma juice flew, and to men brought it through without falter or fail?
Why the Hawk 'twas again, and great Indra to men would appear, now and then, in the shape of a Quail,
While the Thlinkeet's delight is the Bird of the Night, the beak and the bright ebon plumage of Yehl.{8}
And who for man's need brought the famed Suttung's mead? why 'tis told in the creed of the Sagamen strong,
'Twas the Eagle god who brought the drink from the blue, and gave mortals the brew that's the fountain of song. {9}
Next, who gave men their laws? and what reason or cause the young brave overawes when in need of a squaw,
Till he thinks it a shame to wed one of his name, and his conduct you blame if he thus breaks the law?
For you still hold it wrong if a lubra {10} belong to the self-

same kobong {11} that is Father of you,
To take HER as a bride to your ebony side; nay, you give her a wide berth; quite right of you, too.
For her father, you know, is YOUR father, the Crow, and no blessing but woe from the wedding would spring.
Well, these rules they were made in the wattle-gum shade, and were strictly obeyed, when the Crow was the King. {12}
Thus on Earth's little ball to the Birds you owe all, yet your gratitude's small for the favours they've done,
And their feathers you pill, and you eat them at will, yes, you plunder and kill the bright birds one by one;
There's a price on their head, and the Dodo is dead, and the Moa has fled from the sight of the sun!

MAN AND THE ASCIDIAN--A MORALITY

"The Ancestor remote of Man,"
Says Darwin, "is th' Ascidian,"
A scanty sort of water-beast
That, ninety million years at least
Before Gorillas came to be,
Went swimming up and down the sea.

Their ancestors the pious praise,
And like to imitate their ways;
How, then, does our first parent live,
What lesson has his life to give?

Th' Ascidian tadpole, young and gay,

Rhymes a la Mode

Doth Life with one bright eye survey,
His consciousness has easy play.
He's sensitive to grief and pain,
Has tail, and spine, and bears a brain,
And everything that fits the state
Of creatures we call vertebrate.
But age comes on; with sudden shock
He sticks his head against a rock!
His tail drops off, his eye drops in,
His brain's absorbed into his skin;
He does not move, nor feel, nor know
The tidal water's ebb and flow,
But still abides, unstirred, alone,
A sucker sticking to a stone.

And we, his children, truly we
In youth are, like the Tadpole, free.
And where we would we blithely go,
Have brains and hearts, and feel and know.
Then Age comes on! To Habit we
Affix ourselves and are not free;
Th' Ascidian's rooted to a rock,
And we are bond-slaves of the clock;
Our rocks are Medicine--Letters--Law,
From these our heads we cannot draw:
Our loves drop off, our hearts drop in,
And daily thicker grows our skin.

Ah, scarce we live, we scarcely know
The wide world's moving ebb and flow,
The clanging currents ring and shock,
But we are rooted to the rock.
And thus at ending of his span,

Blind, deaf, and indolent, does Man
Revert to the Ascidian.

BALLADE OF THE PRIMITIVE JEST

"What did the dark-haired Iberian laugh at before the tall blonde Aryan drove him into the corners of Europe?"--Brander Matthews.

I am an ancient Jest!
Palaeolithic man
In his arboreal nest
The sparks of fun would fan;
My outline did he plan,
And laughed like one possessed,
'Twas thus my course began,
I am a Merry Jest!

I am an early Jest!
Man delved, and built, and span;
Then wandered South and West
The peoples Aryan,
I journeyed in their van;
The Semites, too, confessed, -
From Beersheba to Dan, -
I am a Merry Jest!

I am an ancient Jest,
Through all the human clan,
Red, black, white, free, oppressed,

Hilarious I ran!
I'm found in Lucian,
In Poggio, and the rest,
I'm dear to Moll and Nan!
I am a Merry Jest!

ENVOY

Prince, you may storm and ban -
Joe Millers ARE a pest,
Suppress me if you can!
I am a Merry Jest!

CAMEOS--SONNETS FROM THE ANTIQUE

These versions from classical passages are pretty close to the original, except where compression was needed, as in the sonnets from Pausanias and Apuleius, or where, as in the case of fragments of AEschylus and Sophocles, a little expansion was required.

CAMEOS

The graver by Apollo's shrine,
Before the Gods had fled, would stand,

A shell or onyx in his hand,
To copy there the face divine,
Till earnest touches, line by line,
Had wrought the wonder of the land
Within a beryl's golden band,
Or on some fiery opal fine.
Ah! would that as some ancient ring
To us, on shell or stone, doth bring,
Art's marvels perished long ago,
So I, within the sonnet's space,
The large Hellenic lines might trace,
The statue in the cameo!

HELEN ON THE WALLS--(Iliad, iii. 146.)

Fair Helen to the Scaean portals came,
Where sat the elders, peers of Priamus,
Thymoetas, Hiketaon, Panthous,
And many another of a noble name,
Famed warriors, now in council more of fame.
Always above the gates, in converse thus
They chattered like cicalas garrulous;
Who marking Helen, swore "it is no shame
That armed Achaean knights, and Ilian men
For such a woman's sake should suffer long.
Fair as a deathless goddess seemeth she.
Nay, but aboard the red-prowed ships again
Home let her pass in peace, not working wrong
To us, and children's children yet to be."

THE ISLES OF THE BLESSED

--(Pindar, Fr., 106, 107 (95): B. 4, 129- 130, 109 (97): B. 4, 132)

Now the light of the sun, in the night of the Earth, on the souls of the True
Shines, and their city is girt with the meadow where reigneth the rose;
And deep is the shade of the woods, and the wind that flits o'er them and through
Sings of the sea, and is sweet from the isles where the frankincense blows:
Green is their garden and orchard, with rare fruits golden it glows,
And the souls of the Blessed are glad in the pleasures on Earth that they knew,
And in chariots these have delight, and in dice and in minstrelsy those,
And the savour of sacrifice clings to the altars and rises anew.

But the Souls that Persephone cleanses from ancient pollution and stain,
These at the end of the age be they prince, be they singer, or seer;
These to the world, shall be born as of old, shall be sages again;
These of their hands shall be hardy, shall live, and shall die, and shall hear
Thanks of the people, and songs of the minstrels that praise them

amain,
And their glory shall dwell in the land where they dwelt, while year calls unto year!

DEATH--(AEsch., Fr., 156.)

Of all Gods Death alone
Disdaineth sacrifice:
No man hath found or shown
The gift that Death would prize.
In vain are songs or sighs,
Paaen, or praise, or moan,
Alone beneath the skies
Hath Death no altar-stone!

There is no head so dear
That men would grudge to Death;
Let Death but ask, we give
All gifts that we may live;
But though Death dwells so near,
We know not what he saith.

NYSA--(Soph., Fr., 235; AEsch., Fr., 56.)

On these Nysaean shores divine

The clusters ripen in a day.
At dawn the blossom shreds away;
The berried grapes are green and fine
And full by noon; in day's decline
They're purple with a bloom of grey,
And e'er the twilight plucked are they,
And crushed, by nightfall, into wine.

But through the night with torch in hand
Down the dusk hills the Maenads fare;
The bull-voiced mummers roar and blare,
The muffled timbrels swell and sound,
And drown the clamour of the band
Like thunder moaning underground.

COLONUS--(OEd. Col., 667-705.)

I.

Here be the fairest homes the land can show,
The silvery-cliffed Colonus; always here
The nightingale doth haunt and singeth clear,
For well the deep green gardens doth she know.
Groves of the God, where winds may never blow,
Nor men may tread, nor noontide sun may peer
Among the myriad-berried ivy dear,
Where Dionysus wanders to and fro.

For here he loves to dwell, and here resort

These Nymphs that are his nurses and his court,
And golden eyed beneath the dewy boughs
The crocus burns, and the narcissus fair
Clusters his blooms to crown thy clustered hair,
Demeter, and to wreathe the Maiden's brows!

II.

Yea, here the dew of Heaven upon the grain
Fails never, nor the ceaseless water-spring,
Near neighbour of Cephisus wandering,
That day by day revisiteth the plain.
Nor do the Goddesses the grove disdain,
But chiefly here the Muses quire and sing,
And here they love to weave their dancing ring,
With Aphrodite of the golden rein.

And here there springs a plant that knoweth not
The Asian mead, nor that great Dorian isle,
Unsown, untilled, within our garden plot
It dwells, the grey-leaved olive; ne'er shall guile
Nor force of foemen root it from the spot:
Zeus and Athene guarding it the while!

THE PASSING OF OEDIPOUS--(OEd. Col., 1655-1666.)

How OEdipous departed, who may tell

Save Theseus only? for there neither came
The burning bolt of thunder, and the flame
To blast him into nothing, nor the swell
Of sea-tide spurred by tempest on him fell.
But some diviner herald none may name
Called him, or inmost Earth's abyss became
The painless place where such a soul might dwell.

Howe'er it chanced, untouched of malady,
Unharmed by fear, unfollowed by lament,
With comfort on the twilight way he went,
Passing, if ever man did, wondrously;
From this world's death to life divinely rent,
Unschooled in Time's last lesson, how we die.

THE TAMING OF TYRO--(Soph., Fr., 587.)

(Sidero, the stepmother of Tyro, daughter of Salmoneus, cruelly entreated her in all things, and chiefly in this, that she let sheer her beautiful hair.)

At fierce Sidero's word the thralls drew near,
And shore the locks of Tyro,--like ripe corn
They fell in golden harvest,--but forlorn
The maiden shuddered in her pain and fear,
Like some wild mare that cruel grooms in scorn
Hunt in the meadows, and her mane they sheer,
And drive her where, within the waters clear,

She spies her shadow, and her shame doth mourn.

Ah! hard were he and pitiless of heart
Who marking that wild thing made weak and tame,
Broken, and grieving for her glory gone,
Could mock her grief; but scornfully apart
Sidero stood, and watched a wind that came
And tossed the curls like fire that flew and shone!

TO ARTEMIS--(Hippol., Eurip., 73-87.)

For thee soft crowns in thine untrampled mead
I wove, my lady, and to thee I bear;
Thither no shepherd drives his flocks to feed,
Nor scythe of steel has ever laboured there;
Nay, through the spring among the blossoms fair
The brown bee comes and goes, and with good heed
Thy maiden, Reverence, sweet streams doth lead
About the grassy close that is her care!

Souls only that are gracious and serene
By gift of God, in human lore unread,
May pluck these holy blooms and grasses green
That now I wreathe for thine immortal head,
I that may walk with thee, thyself unseen,
And by thy whispered voice am comforted.

CRITICISM OF LIFE--(Hippol, Eurip .P., 252-266.)

Long life hath taught me many things, and shown
That lukewarm loves for men who die are best,
Weak wine of liking let them mix alone,
Not Love, that stings the soul within the breast;
Happy, who wears his love-bonds lightliest,
Now cherished, now away at random thrown!
Grievous it is for other's grief to moan,
Hard that my soul for thine should lose her rest!

Wise ruling this of life: but yet again
Perchance too rigid diet is not well;
He lives not best who dreads the coming pain
And shunneth each delight desirable:
FLEE THOU EXTREMES, this word alone is plain,
Of all that God hath given to Man to spell!

AMARYLLIS--(Theocritus, Idyll, iii.)

Fair Amaryllis, wilt thou never peep
From forth the cave, and call me, and be mine?
Lo, apples ten I bear thee from the steep,
These didst thou long for, and all these are thine.
Ah, would I were a honey-bee to sweep

Through ivy, and the bracken, and woodbine;
To watch thee waken, Love, and watch thee sleep,
Within thy grot below the shadowy pine.
Now know I Love, a cruel god is he,
The wild beast bare him in the wild wood drear;
And truly to the bone he burneth me.
But, black-browed Amaryllis, ne'er a tear,
Nor sigh, nor blush, nor aught have I from thee;
Nay, nor a kiss, a little gift and dear.

THE CANNIBAL ZEUS--A.D. 160

[Greek text]--Paus. viii. 38

None elder city doth the Sun behold
Than ancient Lycosura; 'twas begun
Ere Zeus the meat of mortals learned to shun,
And here hath he a grove whose haunted fold
The driven deer seek and huntsmen dread: 'tis told
That whoso fares within that forest dun
Thenceforth shall cast no shadow in the Sun,
Ay, and within the year his life is cold!

Hard by dwelt he {13} who, while the Gods deigned eat
At good men's tables, gave them dreadful meat,
A child he slew: --his mountain altar green
Here still hath Zeus, with rites untold of me,
Piteous, but as they are let these things be,

And as from the beginning they have been!

INVOCATION OF ISIS--(Apuleius, Metamorph. XI.)

Thou that art sandalled on immortal feet
With leaves of palm, the prize of Victory;
Thou that art crowned with snakes and blossoms sweet,
Queen of the silver dews and shadowy sky,
I pray thee by all names men name thee by!
Demeter, come, and leave the yellow wheat!
Or Aphrodite, let thy lovers sigh!
Or Dian, from thine Asian temple fleet!

Or, yet more dread, divine Persephone
From worlds of wailing spectres, ah, draw near;
Approach, Selene, from thy subject sea;
Come, Artemis, and this night spare the deer:
By all thy names and rites I summon thee;
By all thy rites and names, Our Lady, hear!

THE COMING OF ISIS

So Lucius prayed, and sudden, from afar,
Floated the locks of Isis, shone the bright

Crown that is tressed with berry, snake, and star;
She came in deep blue raiment of the night,
Above her robes that now were snowy white,
Now golden as the moons of harvest are,
Now red, now flecked with many a cloudy bay,
Now stained with all the lustre of the light.

Then he who saw her knew her, and he knew
The awful symbols borne in either hand;
The golden urn that laves Demeter's dew,
The handles wreathed with asps, the mystic wand;
The shaken seistron's music, tinkling through
The temples of that old Osirian land.

THE SPINET

My heart an old Spinet with strings
To laughter chiefly turned, but some
That Fate has practised hard on, dumb,
They answer not whoever sings.
The ghosts of half-forgotten things
Will touch the keys with fingers numb,
The little mocking spirits come
And thrill it with their fairy wings.

A jingling harmony it makes
My heart, my lyre, my old Spinet,
And now a memory it wakes,
And now the music means "forget,"

And little heed the player takes
Howe'er the thoughtful critic fret.

NOTES

The Fortunate Islands.

This piece is a rhymed loose version of a passage in the Vera Historia of Lucian. The humorist was unable to resist the temptation to introduce passages of mockery, which are here omitted. Part of his description of the Isles of the Blest has a close and singular resemblance to the New Jerusalem of the Apocalypse. The clear River of Life and the prodigality of gold and of precious stones may especially be noticed.

WHOSO DOTH TASTE THE DEAD MEN'S BREAD, &.c. This belief that the living may visit, on occasion, the dwellings of the dead, but can never return to earth if they taste the food of the departed, is expressed in myths of worldwide distribution. Because she ate the pomegranate seed, Persephone became subject to the spell of Hades. In Apuleius, Psyche, when she visits the place of souls, is advised to abstain from food. Kohl found the myth among the Ojibbeways, Mr. Codrington among the Solomon Islanders; it occurs in Samoa, in the Finnish Kalewala (where Wainamoinen, in Pohjola, refrains from touching meat or drink), and the belief has left its mark on the mediaeval ballad of Thomas of Ercildoune. When he is in Fairy Land, the Fairy Queen supplies him with the bread and wine of earth, and will not suffer him to touch the fruits which grow "in this countrie." See also "Wandering Willie" in Redgauntlet.

AS NOW THE HUTTED ESKIMO. The Eskimo and the miserable Fuegians are almost the only Socialists who practise what European Anarchists preach. The Fuegians go so far as to tear up any piece of cloth which one of the tribe may receive, so that each member may have a rag. The Eskimo are scarcely such consistent walkers, and canoes show a tendency to accumulate in the hands of proprietors. Formerly no Eskimo was allowed to possess more than one canoe. Such was the wild justice of the Polar philosophers.

THE LATEST MINSTREL. "The sound of all others dearest to his ear, the gentle ripple of Tweed over its pebbles, was distinctly audible as we knelt around the bed and his eldest son kissed and closed his eyes."--Lockhart's Life of Scott, vii., 394.

RONSARD'S GRAVE. This version ventures to condense the original which, like most of the works of the Pleiad, is unnecessarily long.

THE SNOW, AND WIND, AND HAIL. Ronsard's rendering of the famous passage in Odyssey, vi., about the dwellings of the Olympians. The vision of a Paradise of learned lovers and poets constantly recurs in the poetry of Joachim du Bellay, and of Ronsard.

ROMANCE. Suggested by a passage in La Faustin, by M. E. de Goncourt, a curious moment of poetry in a repulsive piece of naturalisme.

M. BOULMIER, author of Les Villanelles, died shortly after this villanelle was written; he had not published a larger collection on which he had been at work.

EDMUND GORLIOT. The bibliophile will not easily procure Gorliot's book, which is not in the catalogues. Throughout The Last Maying there is reference to the Pervigilium Veneris.

BIRD-GODS. Apparently Aristophanes preserved, in a burlesque form, the remnants of a genuine myth. Almost all savage religions have their bird-gods, and it is probable that Aristophanes did not invent, but only used a surviving myth of which there are scarcely any other traces in Greek literature.

SPINET. The accent is on the last foot, even when the word is written spinnet. Compare the remarkable Liberty which Pamela took with the 137th Psalm.

My Joys and Hopes all overthrown,
My Heartstrings almost broke,
Unfit my Mind for Melody,
Much more to bear a Joke.
But yet, if from my Innocence
I, even in Thought, should slide,
Then, let my fingers quite forget
The sweet Spinnet to guide!

Pamela, or Virtue Rewarded, vol. i., p. 184., 1785

Notes:

{1} N.B. There is only one veracious statement in this ballade, which must not be accepted as autobiographical.

{2} These lines do NOT apply to Miss Annie P. (or Daisy) Miller, and her delightful sisters, Gades aditurae mecum, in the pocket edition of Mr. James's novels, if ever I go to Gades.

{3} Tonatiu, the Thunder Bird; well known to the Dacotahs and Zulus.

{4} The Hawk, in the myth of the Galinameros of Central California, lit up the Sun.

{5} Pundjel, the Eagle Hawk, is the demiurge and "culture-hero" of several Australian tribes.

{6} The Creation of Man is thus described by the Australians.

{7} In Andaman, Thlinkeet, Melanesian, and other myths, a Bird is the Prometheus Purphoros; in Normandy this part is played by the Wren.

{8} Yehl: the Raven God of the Thlinkeets.

{9} Indra stole Soma as a Hawk and as a Quail. For Odin's feat as a Bird, see Bragi's Telling in the Younger Edda.

{10} Pundjel, the Eagle Hawk, gave Australians their marriage laws.

{11} Lubra, a woman; kobong, "totem;" or, to please Mr. Max Muller, "otem."

{12} The Crow was the Hawk's rival.

{13} Lycaon, the first werewolf.

www.bookjungle.com *email: sales@bookjungle.com fax: 630-214-0564 mail: Book Jungle PO Box 2226 Champaign, IL 61825*

The Codes Of Hammurabi And Moses
W. W. Davies

QTY

The discovery of the Hammurabi Code is one of the greatest achievements of archaeology, and is of paramount interest, not only to the student of the Bible, but also to all those interested in ancient history...

Religion   ISBN: *1-59462-338-4*   Pages:132
MSRP *$12.95*

The Theory of Moral Sentiments
Adam Smith

QTY

This work from 1749. contains original theories of conscience amd moral judgment and it is the foundation for systemof morals.

Philosophy   ISBN: *1-59462-777-0*   Pages:536
MSRP *$19.95*

Jessica's First Prayer
Hesba Stretton

QTY

In a screened and secluded corner of one of the many railway-bridges which span the streets of London there could be seen a few years ago, from five o'clock every morning until half past eight, a tidily set-out coffee-stall, consisting of a trestle and board, upon which stood two large tin cans, with a small fire of charcoal burning under each so as to keep the coffee boiling during the early hours of the morning when the work-people were thronging into the city on their way to their daily toil...

Childrens   ISBN: *1-59462-373-2*   Pages:84
MSRP *$9.95*

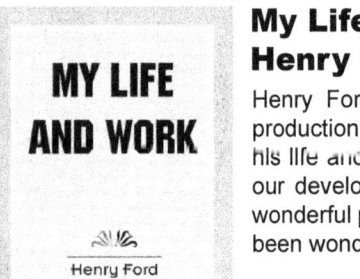

My Life and Work
Henry Ford

QTY

Henry Ford revolutionized the world with his implementation of mass production for the Model T automobile. Gain valuable business insight into his life and work with his own auto-biography... "We have only started on our development of our country we have not as yet, with all our talk of wonderful progress, done more than scratch the surface. The progress has been wonderful enough but..."

Biographies/   ISBN: *1-59462-198-5*   Pages:300
MSRP *$21.95*

www.bookjungle.com *email: sales@bookjungle.com fax: 630-214-0564 mail: Book Jungle PO Box 2226 Champaign, IL 61825*

The Art of Cross-Examination
Francis Wellman

I presume it is the experience of every author, after his first book is published upon an important subject, to be almost overwhelmed with a wealth of ideas and illustrations which could readily have been included in his book, and which to his own mind, at least, seem to make a second edition inevitable. Such certainly was the case with me; and when the first edition had reached its sixth impression in five months, I rejoiced to learn that it seemed to my publishers that the book had met with a sufficiently favorable reception to justify a second and considerably enlarged edition. ..

Reference   ISBN: *1-59462-647-2*   Pages:412 MSRP *$19.95*

On the Duty of Civil Disobedience
Henry David Thoreau

Thoreau wrote his famous essay, On the Duty of Civil Disobedience, as a protest against an unjust but popular war and the immoral but popular institution of slave-owning. He did more than write—he declined to pay his taxes, and was hauled off to gaol in consequence. Who can say how much this refusal of his hastened the end of the war and of slavery?

Law   ISBN: *1-59462-747-9*   Pages:48 MSRP *$7.45*

Dream Psychology Psychoanalysis for Beginners
Sigmund Freud

Sigmund Freud, born Sigismund Schlomo Freud (May 6, 1856 - September 23, 1939), was a Jewish-Austrian neurologist and psychiatrist who co-founded the psychoanalytic school of psychology. Freud is best known for his theories of the unconscious mind, especially involving the mechanism of repression; his redefinition of sexual desire as mobile and directed towards a wide variety of objects; and his therapeutic techniques, especially his understanding of transference in the therapeutic relationship and the presumed value of dreams as sources of insight into unconscious desires.

Psychology   ISBN: *1-59462-905-6*   Pages:196 MSRP *$15.45*

The Miracle of Right Thought
Orison Swett Marden

Believe with all of your heart that you will do what you were made to do. When the mind has once formed the habit of holding cheerful, happy, prosperous pictures, it will not be easy to form the opposite habit. It does not matter how improbable or how far away this realization may see, or how dark the prospects may be, if we visualize them as best we can, as vividly as possible, hold tenaciously to them and vigorously struggle to attain them, they will gradually become actualized, realized in the life. But a desire, a longing without endeavor, a yearning abandoned or held indifferently will vanish without realization.

Self Help   ISBN: *1-59462-644-8*   Pages:360 MSRP *$25.45* www.bookjungle.com email: sales@bookjungle.com fax: 630-214-0564 mail: Book Jungle PO Box 2226 Champaign, IL 61825

QTY

	Title	ISBN	Price
☐	**The Rosicrucian Cosmo-Conception Mystic Christianity** by *Max Heindel*	ISBN: 1-59462-188-8	$38.95

The Rosicrucian Cosmo-conception is not dogmatic, neither does it appeal to any other authority than the reason of the student. It is: not controversial, but is: sent forth in the, hope that it may help to clear...
New Age/Religion Pages 646

☐ **Abandonment To Divine Providence** by *Jean-Pierre de Caussade* ISBN: 1-59462-228-0 $25.95
"The Rev. Jean Pierre de Caussade was one of the most remarkable spiritual writers of the Society of Jesus in France in the 18th Century. His death took place at Toulouse in 1751. His works have gone through many editions and have been republished...
Inspirational/Religion Pages 400

☐ **Mental Chemistry** by *Charles Haanel* ISBN: 1-59462-192-6 $23.95
Mental Chemistry allows the change of material conditions by combining and appropriately utilizing the power of the mind. Much like applied chemistry creates something new and unique out of careful combinations of chemicals the mastery of mental chemistry...
New Age Pages 354

☐ **The Letters of Robert Browning and Elizabeth Barret Barrett 1845-1846 vol II** ISBN: 1-59462-193-4 $35.95
by *Robert Browning* and *Elizabeth Barrett*
Biographies Pages 596

☐ **Gleanings In Genesis (volume I)** by *Arthur W. Pink* ISBN: 1-59462-130-6 $27.45
Appropriately has Genesis been termed "the seed plot of the Bible" for in it we have, in germ form, almost all of the great doctrines which are afterwards fully developed in the books of Scripture which follow...
Religion/Inspirational Pages 420

☐ **The Master Key** by *L. W. de Laurence* ISBN: 1-59462-001-6 $30.95
In no branch of human knowledge has there been a more lively increase of the spirit of research during the past few years than in the study of Psychology, Concentration and Mental Discipline. The requests for authentic lessons in Thought Control, Mental Discipline and...
New Age/Business Pages 422

☐ **The Lesser Key Of Solomon Goetia** by *L. W. de Laurence* ISBN: 1-59462-092-X $9.95
This translation of the first book of the "Lernegton" which is now for the first time made accessible to students of Talismanic Magic was done, after careful collation and edition, from numerous Ancient Manuscripts in Hebrew, Latin, and French...
New Age/Occult Pages 92

☐ **Rubaiyat Of Omar Khayyam** by *Edward Fitzgerald* ISBN:1-59462-332-5 $13.95
Edward Fitzgerald, whom he would have already learned, in spite of his own efforts to remain within the shadow of anonymity, to look upon as one of the rarest poets of the century, was born at Bredfield, in Suffolk, on the 31st of March, 1809. He was the third son of John Purcell...
Music Pages 172

☐ **Ancient Law** by *Henry Maine* ISBN: 1-59462-128-4 $29.95
The chief object of the following pages is to indicate some of the earliest ideas of mankind, as they are reflected in Ancient Law, and to point out the relation of those ideas to modern thought.
Religion/History Pages 452

☐ **Far-Away Stories** by *William J. Locke* ISBN: 1-59462-129-2 $19.45
"Good wine needs no bush, but a collection of mixed vintages does. And this book is just such a collection. Some of the stories I do not want to remain buried for ever in the museum files of dead magazine-numbers an author's not unpardonable vanity..."
Fiction Pages 272

☐ **Life of David Crockett** by *David Crockett* ISBN: 1-59462-250-7 $27.45
"Colonel David Crockett was one of the most remarkable men of the times in which he lived. Born in humble life, but gifted with a strong will, an indomitable courage, and unremitting perseverance...
Biographies/New Age Pages 424

☐ **Lip-Reading** by *Edward Nitchie* ISBN: 1-59462-206-X $25.95
Edward B. Nitchie, founder of the New York School for the Hard of Hearing, now the Nitchie School of Lip-Reading, Inc, wrote "LIP-READING Principles and Practice". The development and perfecting of this meritorious work on lip-reading was an undertaking...
How-to Pages 400

☐ **A Handbook of Suggestive Therapeutics, Applied Hypnotism, Psychic Science** ISBN: 1-59462-214-0 $24.95
by *Henry Munro*
Health/New Age/Health/Self-help Pages 376

☐ **A Doll's House: and Two Other Plays** by *Henrik Ibsen* ISBN: 1-59462-112-8 $19.95
Henrik Ibsen created this classic when in revolutionary 1848 Rome. Introducing some striking concepts in playwriting for the realist genre, this play has been studied the world over.
Fiction/Classics/Plays 308

☐ **The Light of Asia** by *sir Edwin Arnold* ISBN: 1-59462-204-3 $13.95
In this poetic masterpiece, Edwin Arnold describes the life and teachings of Buddha. The man who was to become known as Buddha to the world was born as Prince Gautama of India but he rejected the worldly riches and abandoned the reigns of power when...
Religion/History/Biographies Pages 170

☐ **The Complete Works of Guy de Maupassant** by *Guy de Maupassant* ISBN: 1-59462-157-8 $16.95
"For days and days, nights and nights, I had dreamed of that first kiss which was to consecrate our engagement, and I knew not on what spot I should put my lips..."
Fiction/Classics Pages 240

☐ **The Art of Cross-Examination** by *Francis L. Wellman* ISBN: 1-59462-309-0 $26.95
Written by a renowned trial lawyer, Wellman imparts his experience and uses case studies to explain how to use psychology to extract desired information through questioning.
How-to/Science/Reference Pages 408

☐ **Answered or Unanswered?** by *Louisa Vaughan* ISBN: 1-59462-248-5 $10.95
Miracles of Faith in China
Religion Pages 112

☐ **The Edinburgh Lectures on Mental Science (1909)** by *Thomas* ISBN: 1-59462-008-3 $11.95
This book contains the substance of a course of lectures recently given by the writer in the Queen Street Hall, Edinburgh. Its purpose is to indicate the Natural Principles governing the relation between Mental Action and Material Conditions...
New Age Psychology Pages 148

☐ **Ayesha** by *H. Rider Haggard* ISBN: 1-59462-301-5 $24.95
Verily and indeed it is the unexpected that happens! Probably if there was one person upon the earth from whom the Editor of this, and of a certain previous history, did not expect to hear again...
Classics Pages 380

☐ **Ayala's Angel** by *Anthony Trollope* ISBN: 1-59462-352-X $29.95
The two girls were both pretty, but Lucy who was twenty-one who supposed to be simple and comparatively unattractive, whereas Ayala was credited, as her Bombwhat romantic name might show, with poetic charm and a taste for romance. Ayala when her father died was nineteen...
Fiction Pages 484

☐ **The American Commonwealth** by *James Bryce* ISBN: 1-59462-286-8 $34.45
An interpretation of American democratic political theory. It examines political mechanics and society from the perspective of Scotsman James Bryce
Politics Pages 572

☐ **Stories of the Pilgrims** by *Margaret P. Pumphrey* ISBN: 1-59462-116-0 $17.95
This book explores pilgrims religious oppression in England as well as their escape to Holland and eventual crossing to America on the Mayflower, and their early days in New England...
History Pages 268

www.bookjungle.com *email:* sales@bookjungle.com *fax:* 630-214-0564 *mail:* Book Jungle PO Box 2226 Champaign, IL 61825

QTY

The Fasting Cure by *Sinclair Upton* ISBN: *1-59462-222-1* **$13.95**
In the Cosmopolitan Magazine for May, 1910, and in the Contemporary Review (London) for April, 1910, I published an article dealing with my experiences in fasting. I have written a great many magazine articles, but never one which attracted so much attention... New Age/Self Help/Health Pages 164

Hebrew Astrology by *Sepharial* ISBN: *1-59462-308-2* **$13.45**
In these days of advanced thinking it is a matter of common observation that we have left many of the old landmarks behind and that we are now pressing forward to greater heights and to a wider horizon than that which represented the mind-content of our progenitors... Astrology Pages 144

Thought Vibration or The Law of Attraction in the Thought World ISBN: *1-59462-127-6* **$12.95**
by *William Walker Atkinson* Psychology/Religion Pages 144

Optimism by *Helen Keller* ISBN: *1-59462-108-X* **$15.95**
Helen Keller was blind, deaf, and mute since 19 months old, yet famously learned how to overcome these handicaps, communicate with the world, and spread her lectures promoting optimism. An inspiring read for everyone... Biographies/Inspirational Pages 84

Sara Crewe by *Frances Burnett* ISBN: *1-59462-360-0* **$9.45**
In the first place, Miss Minchin lived in London. Her home was a large, dull, tall one, in a large, dull square, where all the houses were alike, and all the sparrows were alike, and where all the door-knockers made the same heavy sound... Childrens/Classic Pages 88

The Autobiography of Benjamin Franklin by *Benjamin Franklin* ISBN: *1-59462-135-7* **$24.95**
The Autobiography of Benjamin Franklin has probably been more extensively read than any other American historical work, and no other book of its kind has had such ups and downs of fortune. Franklin lived for many years in England, where he was agent... Biographies/History Pages 332

Name	
Email	
Telephone	
Address	
City, State ZIP	

☐ Credit Card   ☐ Check / Money Order

Credit Card Number	
Expiration Date	
Signature	

Please Mail to: Book Jungle
PO Box 2226
Champaign, IL 61825
or Fax to: 630-214-0564

ORDERING INFORMATION
web: *www.bookjungle.com*
email: *sales@bookjungle.com*
fax: *630-214-0564*
mail: *Book Jungle PO Box 2226 Champaign, IL 61825*
or PayPal *to sales@bookjungle.com*

Please contact us for bulk discounts

DIRECT-ORDER TERMS

20% Discount if You Order Two or More Books
Free Domestic Shipping!
Accepted: Master Card, Visa, Discover, American Express

www.ingramcontent.com/pod-product-compliance
Lightning Source LLC
Chambersburg PA
CBHW081325040426

42453CB00013B/2307